I0796853

This book belongs to:

If found, please contact

EMAIL:

PHONE:

Must-Read Classics

A BOOK CLUB JOURNAL FOR BIBLIOPHILES

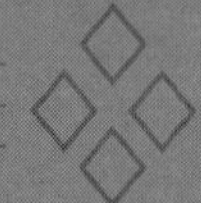

"I have always imagined that Paradise will be a kind of library."

—JORGE LUIS BORGES

INTRODUCTION

Whether you are part of a book club, thinking of starting an informal reading group, or simply want to chat about books with a friend, writing about what you're reading is an essential tool to help you clarify your thinking and insights and, most important, grow your enjoyment.

While this journal is designed to specifically help you read, write about, and discuss classic literature from around the world, these pages can be used as a template to think about any book. Inside, you'll find pages to record thoughts off-the-cuff as you read, as well as sample questions that can help guide your book club discussions and ample space for recording notes and ideas that come up as you discuss with others.

You'll also get a list of "must-read" classic works pulled from both the traditional Western canon as well as beloved writers and works from non-Western cultures and traditions. Take this list along to your favorite bookstore or library when picking your next read or share it with your book club and put it to a vote!

We can't guarantee that you'll love every book that is considered a classic—as Mark Twain famously said, "A classic is something that everybody wants to have read and nobody wants to read"—but you will be challenged and engaged by each of them. And as you write and share your thoughts about them, you will be entering the centuries-long conversation about what these great works say about the human condition.

Have fun! And make sure to bring a snack!

CLASSIC BOOKS TO READ

This list is by no means exhaustive! Ask librarians and booksellers, too.

	READ	REREAD
Pride and Prejudice *by Jane Austen*	○	○
To Kill a Mockingbird *by Harper Lee*	○	○
1984 *by George Orwell*	○	○
Jane Eyre *by Charlotte Brontë*	○	○
The Great Gatsby *by F. Scott Fitzgerald*	○	○
The Odyssey *by Homer*	○	○
Journey to the West *by Wu Cheng'en*	○	○
Don Quixote *by Miguel de Cervantes*	○	○
Frankenstein *by Mary Wollstonecraft Shelley*	○	○
Bel Canto *by Ann Patchett*	○	○
Germinal *by Émile Zola*	○	○
One Hundred Years of Solitude *by Gabriel García Márquez*	○	○
Treasure Island *by Robert Louis Stevenson*	○	○
Camilla *by Frances Burney*	○	○
Martin Eden *by Jack London*	○	○
Efuru *by Flora Nwapa*	○	○
O Pioneers! *by Willa Cather*	○	○
Tristram Shandy *by Laurence Sterne*	○	○

	READ	REREAD
The Adventures of Huckleberry Finn *by Mark Twain*	○	○
The Scarlet Letter *by Nathaniel Hawthorne*	○	○
Moby-Dick *by Herman Melville*	○	○
The Death of the Heart *by Elizabeth Bowen*	○	○
Madame Bovary *by Gustave Flaubert*	○	○
Little Women *by Louisa May Alcott*	○	○
Great Expectations *by Charles Dickens*	○	○
The Secret History *by Donna Tartt*	○	○
The Way We Live Now *by Anthony Trollope*	○	○
The Brothers Karamazov *by Fyodor Dostoevsky*	○	○
The Picture of Dorian Gray *by Oscar Wilde*	○	○
As I Lay Dying *by William Faulkner*	○	○
Wise Blood *by Flannery O'Connor*	○	○
The Beautiful Ones Are Not Yet Born *by Ayi Kwei Armah*	○	○
The Tenant of Wildfell Hall *by Anne Brontë*	○	○
Robinson Crusoe *by Daniel Defoe*	○	○
Their Eyes Were Watching God *by Zora Neale Hurston*	○	○
A Farewell to Arms *by Ernest Hemingway*	○	○
The Talented Mr. Ripley *by Patricia Highsmith*	○	○
On the Road *by Jack Kerouac*	○	○
The Woman in White *by Wilkie Collins*	○	○

	READ	REREAD
Rebecca *by Daphne du Maurier*	○	○
The Bell Jar *by Sylvia Plath*	○	○
The Color Purple *by Alice Walker*	○	○
Anna Karenina *by Leo Tolstoy*	○	○
Charlotte's Web *by E. B. White*	○	○
Dracula *by Bram Stoker*	○	○
The Grapes of Wrath *by John Steinbeck*	○	○
Fear of Flying *by Erica Jong*	○	○
Invisible Man *by Ralph Ellison*	○	○
Les Misérables *by Victor Hugo*	○	○
North and South *by Elizabeth Gaskell*	○	○
Beloved *by Toni Morrison*	○	○
A Portrait of the Artist as a Young Man *by James Joyce*	○	○
The Yellow Wallpaper *by Charlotte Perkins Gilman*	○	○
The Return of the Native *by Thomas Hardy*	○	○
The Big Sleep *by Raymond Chandler*	○	○
The Sea, the Sea *by Iris Murdoch*	○	○
I, Claudius *by Robert Graves*	○	○
Mrs. Dalloway *by Virginia Woolf*	○	○
Wuthering Heights *by Emily Brontë*	○	○

	READ	REREAD
Another Country *by James Baldwin*	○	○
Alice's Adventures in Wonderland *by Lewis Carroll*	○	○
Vanity Fair *by William Makepeace Thackeray*	○	○
Persuasion *by Jane Austen*	○	○
Under the Volcano *by Malcolm Lowry*	○	○
The Way of All Flesh *by Samuel Butler*	○	○
The Heart Is a Lonely Hunter *by Carson McCullers*	○	○
Native Son *by Richard Wright*	○	○
Winesburg, Ohio *by Sherwood Anderson*	○	○
We Have Always Lived in the Castle *by Shirley Jackson*	○	○
The Wings of the Dove *by Henry James*	○	○
A Handful of Dust *by Evelyn Waugh*	○	○
A Room with a View *by E. M. Forster*	○	○
The House of the Spirits *by Isabel Allende*	○	○
The Joy Luck Club *by Amy Tan*	○	○
The Age of Innocence *by Edith Wharton*	○	○
Beowulf *by unknown*	○	○
The Count of Monte Cristo *by Alexandre Dumas*	○	○
Outlaws of the Marsh *by Shi Nai'an*	○	○
The Promised Land *by Grace Ogot*	○	○

WHAT TO WRITE ABOUT WHEN YOU WRITE ABOUT BOOKS

As you plan discussions about the book you've chosen, use these questions to help guide your thinking and steer the conversations in interesting ways. Refer to these both as you record your personal thoughts and during your book club or casual discussions.

- What did you know about this classic work before you read it? Is this the first time you've tried to read it?
- Do you find the writing style accessible and easy to follow?
- As you read, highlight passages that strike you as beautiful or interesting. Pick one of these passages and describe what makes it important to you.
- What do you know about the biography of the author of this work? Does your knowledge (or lack thereof) contribute to how you think about the work?
- What character in this work do you most connect with?
- Does this book seem to have a "moral" or "lesson"? Do you feel it applies to life today?
- What is the core theme of the book? How is that illuminated through the actions of the characters?
- Are there any depictions or stereotypes in this classic work that strike you as troubling or out-of-date to a modern reader?
- What surprised you about this work?
- Try to find a single quote from the book that sums up the overall theme.
- What makes this book special? The story? The language? The characters?
- If you were to recommend this book to someone else, what would you tell them about it?
- If you disliked the work, what were your key reasons for feeling that way?
- Have you read other works by this author? How do they compare?
- What themes in the book seem universal, and what themes feel rooted in the time and place of the book's conception?

BOOK:

DATE:

BOOK:
DATE:

BOOK:

DATE:

BOOK:

DATE:

BOOK:

DATE:

CHARACTER STUDY

Who is your favorite character in this book?

Name:

Explain what makes them interesting. Do they remind you of anyone in your own life?

BOOK:

DATE:

BOOK:

DATE:

BOOK:

DATE:

BOOK:

DATE:

BOOK:

DATE:

BOOK:

DATE:

BOOK:

DATE:

BOOK:

DATE:

"Many a book
is like a key to
unknown
chambers within
the castle of one's
own self."

—FRANZ KAFKA

SUPERLATIVE

Write down your favorite sentence from this book that you've read thus far:

Page #:

What makes this sentence so extraordinary?

BOOK:

DATE:

BOOK:

DATE:

BOOK:

DATE:

BOOK:

DATE:

BOOK:

DATE:

BOOK:

DATE:

BOOK:

DATE:

BOOK:

DATE:

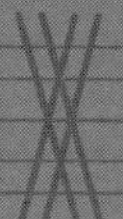

"We are of opinion that instead of letting books grow moldy behind an iron grating, far from the vulgar gaze, it is better to let them wear out by being read."

—JULES VERNE

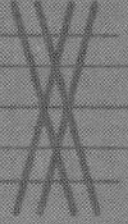

BOOK:
DATE:

BOOK:

DATE:

BOOK:

DATE:

BOOK:

DATE:

"You can never
get a cup of tea
large enough
or a book
long enough
to suit me."

—C. S. LEWIS

BOOK:

DATE:

BOOK:

DATE:

BOOK:

DATE:

BOOK:
DATE:

BOOK:

DATE:

BOOK:

DATE:

If you could ask the author of this book one question, what would it be?

What do you think they would say?

BOOK:
DATE:

BOOK:

DATE:

BOOK:

DATE:

BOOK:

DATE:

BOOK:

DATE:

BOOK:

DATE:

"Books serve to
show a man
that those original
thoughts of his
aren't very new
after all."

—ABRAHAM LINCOLN

BOOK:
DATE:

BOOK:
DATE:

BOOK:

DATE:

BOOK:

DATE:

BOOK:

DATE:

BOOK:

DATE:

BOOK:

DATE:

BOOK:

DATE:

"There is no Frigate
like a Book
To take us
Lands away."

—EMILY DICKINSON

BOOK:

DATE:

BOOK:

DATE:

BOOK:

DATE:

BOOK:

DATE:

BOOK:

DATE:

BOOK:

DATE:

BOOK:

DATE:

BOOK:

DATE:

BOOK:

DATE:

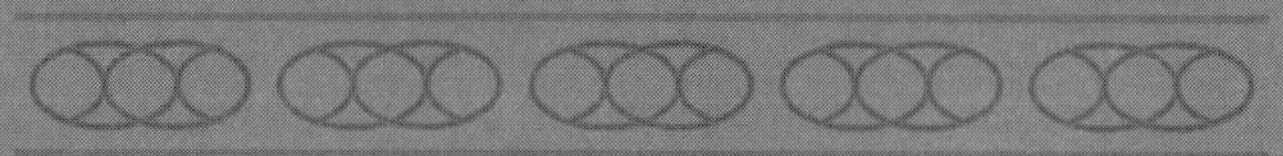

“Some books
leave us free
and
some books
make us free.”

—RALPH WALDO EMERSON

BOOK:

DATE:

BOOK:

DATE:

BOOK:

DATE:

BOOK:

DATE:

BOOK:
DATE:

VIBE CHECK

Is this book overrated or underrated?

Why?

BOOK:

DATE:

BOOK:

DATE:

BOOK:

DATE:

BOOK:

DATE:

BOOK:

DATE:

BOOK:

DATE:

BOOK:

DATE:

BOOK:

DATE:

STORYTELLING

Did the world of the book feel "real," or did it feel like a story? How immersed were you in the actions of the book?

BOOK:
DATE:

BOOK:

DATE:

BOOK:

DATE:

BOOK:

DATE:

BOOK:

DATE:

BOOK:

DATE:

BOOK:

DATE:

BOOK:

DATE:

BOOK:

DATE:

LOOK-ALIKES

Do any characters in the book remind you of other characters from fiction, TV, or movies? Write a few sentences describing the similarities.

BOOK:

DATE:

BOOK:

DATE:

BOOK:

DATE:

BOOK:

DATE:

BOOK:

DATE:

BOOK:

DATE:

BOOK:

DATE:

BOOK:

DATE:

CASTING CALL

If this book were to be turned into a new film, which actors would you cast in the roles?

BOOK:

DATE:

BOOK:

DATE:

BOOK:

DATE:

BOOK:

DATE:

BOOK:

DATE:

"It was books
that taught me that
the things that
tormented me most
were the very things
that connected me
with all the people
who were alive, or who
had ever been alive."

—JAMES BALDWIN

BOOK:
DATE:

BOOK:

DATE:

BOOK:

DATE:

BOOK:

DATE:

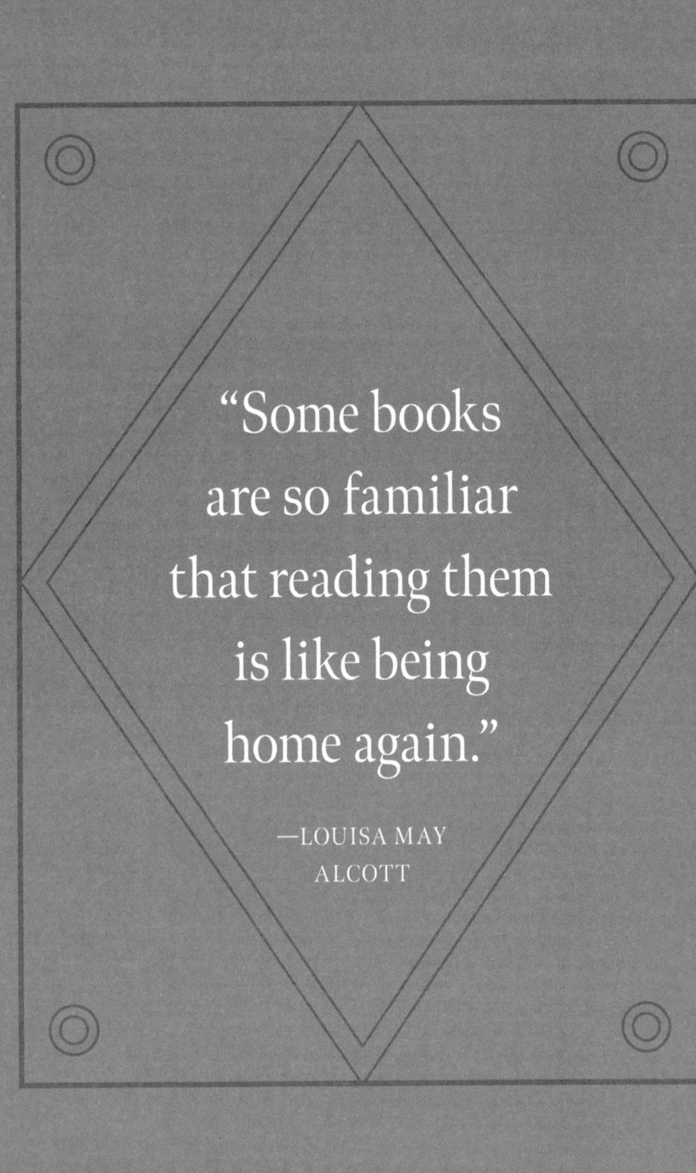
"Some books are so familiar that reading them is like being home again."
—LOUISA MAY ALCOTT

BOOK:
DATE:

BOOK:

DATE:

BOOK:
DATE:

BOOK:

DATE:

BOOK:

DATE:

BOOK:

DATE:

BEGINNINGS

Was this a slow start, or did you get pulled into the tale instantly?

BOOK:

DATE:

BOOK:

DATE:

BOOK:

DATE:

BOOK:

DATE:

FIRST AND LAST

When you finish the book, come to this space and write the first sentence of the work and the last. What do these two sentences make you feel about the book?

BOOK:

DATE:

BOOK:

DATE:

BOOK:

DATE:

BOOK:

DATE:

BOOK:

DATE:

BOOK:

DATE:

AFTER-PARTY

What do you think happened to the characters after the end of the book?

BOOK:

DATE:

BOOK:

DATE:

BOOK:

DATE:

BOOK:

DATE:

CHANGES

If you could change one thing about the book, what would it be? The plot? The pacing? The ending?

BOOK:

DATE:

BOOK:

DATE:

BOOK:

DATE:

BOOK:

DATE:

BOOK:

DATE:

BOOK:
DATE:

“A book, too,
can be a star,
a living fire to
lighten the darkness,
leading out into the
expanding universe.”

—MADELEINE L’ENGLE

BOOK:

DATE:

BOOK:

DATE:

BOOK:

DATE:

BOOK:

DATE:

"It is what you read
when you don't have to
that determines what
you will be when
you can't help it."

—OSCAR WILDE

BOOK:

DATE:

BOOK:
DATE:

BOOK:

DATE:

BOOK:

DATE:

BOOK:

DATE:

UNION SQUARE & CO. and the distinctive Union Square & Co. Gift logo are trademarks of Sterling Publishing Co., Inc.

Union Square & Co., LLC, is a subsidiary of Sterling Publishing Co., Inc.

ISBN 978-1-4549-6002-7

For information about custom editions, special sales, and premium purchases, please contact specialsales@unionsquareandco.com.

Printed in India

2 4 6 8 10 9 7 5 3 1

unionsquareandco.com

Interior design by Christine Heun

Cover design by Igor Satanovsky and Kaylie Pendleton

Cover and interior art: Annetka/iStock/Getty Images Plus; marbled endpaper background: Andy Magee/Shutterstock.com